Celebration Designs

Christmas Candle; see page 34.

Lorraine Sorby-Howlett
&
Marian Jones

CHILD & ASSOCIATES
AN ALL-AUSTRALIAN PUBLISHER

Wonderful Gift; see page 47.

Published by Child & Associates Publishing Pty Ltd,
5 Skyline Place, Frenchs Forest, NSW, Australia, 2086
Co-published outside Australia and New Zealand by
Merehurst Press
5 Great James Street, London WC1N 3DA, England
This book has been edited, designed and typeset in Australia
by the Publisher
First Edition 1988
Text by Lorraine Sorby-Howlett and Marian Jones
Photography by Lennart Osbeck
© Lorraine Sorby-Howlett and Marian Jones 1988
Printed in Singapore by Toppan Printing Co. (S) Pte Ltd

**National Library of Australia
Cataloguing-in-Publication**

Sorby-Howlett, Lorraine
    Celebration designs.

    ISBN 0 86777 117 8.

    1. Cake decorating. I. Jones, Marian.
    II. Title.

641.8'653

Contents

INTRODUCTION

One never loses that special sense of wonder in watching a craftsperson at work. I have had the privilege of watching two such craftspeople in Lorraine Sorby-Howlett and Marian Jones preparing their art for this, their third book, *Celebration Designs*.

We often wish to express our thoughts and love for that very special celebration but somehow lack either the skill or imagination to project our feelings when the day comes. It may not be that the talent isn't there—just the spark to make the idea a reality.

However Lorraine and Marian once again show us how to bring our ideas into being with their clues and talented suggestions. The true reward of a successful book is the comment 'I can do that' or 'Why didn't I think of that?'. Well, now you can do it easily and quickly.

I am very proud to suggest the addition of *Celebration Designs* to your cake decorating library. Whether you are a novice or an expert, the ideas are practical, pretty and simple for that special day.

Marina J. Bradley
Sanctuary Point

FLORAL BASKET

An interesting side design in this eye-catching cake teams well with a pretty basket of flowers which can be removed and kept as a memento.

You will need:

To bake	1 medium five-scalloped cake
Board	Allow 5 cm (2 inch) larger all round than cake
Flowers	4 miniature frangipanis 5 *Kurume* azaleas 6 bunches of hyacinths
Ribbons	5 bunches of loops
Special Effect:	1 flower basket

HAWAIIAN PEARL

A unique cake for that special event. The cake was baked in a special round tin and the shell has been moulded in modelling paste.

You will need:

To bake	Round ball cake
Board	32 x 25 cm (13 x 10 inch) rectangle
Flowers	1 hibiscus
	1 bud
	3 leaves

GOLDEN DAYS

When you reach that magical fifty years of marriage you should have a very special cake for the celebration. The tones have been kept in the cream, yellow, and gold that befits this golden anniversary.

You will need:

To bake	20 cm (8 inch) round cake
Board	28 cm (11 inch) round
Flowers	4 daffodils
	10 baby orchids
	6 jasmine
	5 sprays of baby's breath
Ribbons	3 bunches
Special Effect:	1 fan

STRING OF PEARLS

Make her dream world come true with this enchanting cake. A sophisticated cake for that special event. Any wife would be thrilled to receive this as a gift on that memorable day.

You will need:

To bake	1 shallow loaf tin cake
Board	25 cm (10 inch) oblong
Flowers	1 single rose

ROSE MASQUERADE

The gold and apricot tones in the flowers make this a very suitable cake for special occasions such as Mother's Day and golden anniversaries.

You will need:

To bake	1 medium long oval cake
Board	Allow 5 cm (2 inch) larger all round than cake
Flowers	1 large tea rose 4 small tea roses 14 rosebuds 6 sprays of wedding bush
Ribbons	5 bunches 0.5 metre (1/2 yard)
Special Effect:	1 gift card

FOR MY LOVE

A romantic way to show your affection for your loved one. The dainty heart set among the flowers is complemented by the simple side feature of shaded ribbons.

You will need:

To bake	20 cm (8 inch) round cake
Board	28 cm (11 inch) round
Flowers	3 tea roses 2 buds 11 bunches of small cutter flowers 6 large cutter flowers 8 leaves
Ribbons	4 bunches 1 metre (1 yard) for top 3 metres (3 yards) for side 1 metre (1 yard) for bottom
Special Effect:	1 flooded heart

PINK SUPREME

A cake that celebrates any special day. Beautiful flowers, fine embroidery and extension add a delightful finish to this classic beauty.

You will need:

To bake	20 cm (8 inch) round cake
Board	28 cm (11 inch) round
Flowers	8 dog roses 3 carnations 3 fuchsias 5 bunches of hyacinths 5 leaves
Ribbons	6 bunches of loops 2 metres (2 yards)

MOTHER'S DAY

The living card makes a very beautiful top arrangement for this special cake. The colours can be varied to suit mother's preference.

You will need:

To bake	20 cm (8 inch) square cake
Board	28 cm (11 inch) square
Flowers	6 daisies
	6 mini orchids
	6 sprays of baby's breath
Ribbons	4 medium loops

PRETTY ROSE

A delicate cake that will make any occasion a celebration.

You will need:

To bake	1 medium corner cut diamond cake
Board	Allow 5 cm (2 inch) larger all round than cake
Flowers	1 camellia rose 21 sprays of Mexican orange blossom
Ribbons	3 large bunches of shaded colours
Special Effects:	30 medallions for edging 1 metre (1 yard) each of three different shades

MY PRETTY MAID

This pretty lady is ready to go to the ball. Her gown is scooped up at one side so that the beautiful frills and embossing maybe admired.

You will need:

To bake	1 Dolly Varden cake
Board	32 cm (13 inch) round
Flowers	10 *Bouvardia* 6 buds 2 sprays of tiny blossom
Ribbons	1 small bunch of loops for bouquet

THINKING OF YOU

A charming cake for that special person in your thoughts. The design has been made using the jellywork technique. It is sure to be a winner on any occasion.

You will need:

To bake	1 medium oblong cake with the corners cut
Board	Allow 5 cm (2 inch) larger all round than cake
Flowers	3 Cecil Brunner roses 1 large bud 2 smaller buds
Ribbon	1 bow 1.5 metres (1 1/2 yards)

Pattern shown 3/4 of actual size

FATHER'S SPECIAL DAY

Help dad celebrate his special day with a cake that features a beer stein of his favourite brew.

You will need:

To bake	20 cm (8 inch) square cake
Board	28 cm (11 inch) square
Flowers	4 flannel flowers 4 bunches of wattle 6 bunches of gumnuts
Ribbon	1 metre (1 yard)

HERITAGE

When dad's special day arrives delight him with this masculine cake.

You will need:

To bake	20 cm (8 inch) square cake
Board	28 cm (11 inch) square
Ribbons	2 metres (2 yards)

MEADOW SONG

This modern arrangement of twin hearts complete with wishing well and a cascade of spring flowers features lovely lace scallops caught with tiny rosebuds.

You will need:

To bake	2 heart-shaped cakes
Board	Allow 7.5 cm (3 inch) all round larger than cake
Flowers	18 mountain primulas 9 rosebuds 17 leaves
Ribbons	10 bunches
Special Effect:	1 wishing well

LAVENDER AND LACE

Delicate lavender tones have been used on this cake, which would be suitable for an engagement or any special occasion.

You will need:

To bake	23 cm (9 inch) round cake
Board	30 cm (12 inch) round
Flowers	2 briar roses
	5 Singapore orchids
	3 *Kurume* azaleas
	16 cutter flowers
Ribbons	1 bunch
	1.5 metres (1 1/2 yards)
Special Effect:	1 moulded book

SWEETHEARTS

When romance is in the air, this twin heart cake will make a charming centrepiece for the celebration. The scroll is large enough to take individual messages for the engaged couple.

You will need:

To bake	1 twin heart cake
Board	Allow 5 cm (2 inch) larger all round than cake
Flowers	3 orchids 6 sprays of baby's breath
Ribbon	3 large bunches
Special Effect:	1 scroll

HIS AND HERS

A novel cake for a fun loving couple who would like to celebrate their engagement at a fun party.

You will need:

To bake	Round ball cake
	Piece of cake for book
Board	32 x 25 cm (13 x 10 inch) rectangle
	corner cut

HAND-IN-HAND

When that special moment in your life arrives this cake will mark the celebration.

You will need:

To bake	23 cm (9 inch) heart
Board	Allow 7.5 cm (3 inch) larger all round than cake
Flowers	46 cutter flowers 8 blossoms 4 buds 6 sprays of tiny blossom
Ribbons	6 small bunches 2 metres (2 yards)

SPRING GLORY

A dainty dream cake featuring a posy of rose buds and violets nestling in fine lacework.

You will need:

To bake	20 cm (8 inch) round cake
Board	23 cm (11 inch) round board
Flowers	6 Cecil Brunner rosebuds 8 rosebuds 14 violets 17 leaves
Ribbons	2 metres (2 yards) for sides
Special Effect:	6 bunches of tulle

BE MY LOVE

Red roses, a symbol of true love, are used to surround the ring case on this romantic cake.

You will need:

To bake	1 medium scalloped oval cake
Board	Allow 5 cm (2 inch) larger all round than cake
Flowers	21 rose buds 4 sprays of snowdrops 10 leaves 6 sprays of baby's tears
Ribbons	5 bunches 2 metres (2 yards)
Special Effect:	1 ring case with ring

CELEBRATION TIME

A wonderful cake to help you celebrate any special occasion. The moulded clam shell filled with beautiful flowers is suspended above the cake on a clear perspex pillar.

You will need:

To bake	23 cm (9 inch) ring cake
Board	30 cm (12 inch) round
Flowers	20 *Kurume* azaleas 6 sprays of orange blossom 6 sprays of snowdrops 6 bunches of tiny blossoms
Ribbons	5 bunches of gold loops 1 large florist bow
Special Effect:	1 moulded clam shell

SILVER ANNIVERSARY

A simple cake to celebrate your wedding anniversary. This cake would look lovely also for a golden anniversary.

You will need:

To bake	20 cm (8 inch) cake
Board	28 cm (11 inch)
Flowers	23 *Kurume* azaleas 7 sprays of sweet rocket
Ribbons	3 bunches 1 metre (1 yard)

PAGES OF LOVE

This cake is just perfect to celebrate a special anniversary. The page effect is achieved using rice paper. Any combination of flowers and colour shadings can be used.

You will need:

To bake	1 book cake
Board	Allow 7.5 cm (3 inch) larger all round than cake
Flowers	7 frangipanis 6 sprays of hyacinths
Ribbons	3 large bunches of loops 3 small bunches of loops 0.5 metre (1/2 yard) for bookmark

The Marriage

of

Denis and Irene

50 Happy Years

FIRST ANNIVERSARY

Your first anniversary is chimed in by these pretty bells.
Crystal ribbons delightfully complement the delicate
shaded sweet peas.

You will need:

To bake	1 upright bell-shaped cake, cut in half
Board	Oblong, allow 5 cm (2 inch) larger all round than cake
Flowers	10 sweet peas 5 buds
Ribbons	2 large bunches

HEARTS AND FLOWERS

Soft and delicate creams and apricots combine well to make this cake a beautiful centrepiece for that special engagement.

You will need:

To bake	1 medium octagonal cake
Board	Allow 5 cm (2 inch) larger all round than cake
Flowers	24 mountain primula 17 star flowers 16 leaves
Ribbons	9 bunches 2 metres (2 yards)
Special Effects:	2 hearts

NOW TO DREAM

All the thrill of Christmas time is yours when you decorate this enchanting cake. Sure to charm both young and old.

Pattern shown 3/4 of actual size

You will need:

To bake	20 cm (8 inch) round cake
Board	28 cm (11 inch) round
Flowers	Piped fir leaves Holly berries
Special Effect:	Design airbrushed using the frisk film method

AWAY IN A MANGER

Red ribbons are used to form the candle on the side design. It is combined with moulded holly leaves and berries which are also used to frame the dainty painting which is the centrepiece of the design.

You will need:

To bake	20 cm (8 inch) square cake
Board	28 cm (11 inch) square
Flowers	86 holly leaves Berries to suit
Special Effect:	Red ribbon for candles

CHRISTMAS CANDLE

This jolly mouse adds a special effect to the Christmas candle cake. The colours are bright to add to the excitement of the day.

You will need:

To bake	1 nut roll cake
Board	20 cm (8 inch) round
Special Effects:	1 candlestick base
	1 hand-moulded mouse
	Gifts

FESTIVE CRACKER

This colourful cake makes an ideal centrepiece for your festive table.

You will need:

To bake	1 nut roll cake
Board	1 long oval allowing for ends
Flowers	8 sprays of wattle 6 flannel flowers 3 sprays of gum nuts
Ribbons	2 bows

TRIM A TREE

The royal icing collar on this cake frames the picture of Santa trimming your Christmas tree.

You will need:

To bake	1 medium flat bell cake
Board	Allow 5 cm (2 inch larger all round than cake
Ribbon	1 large florist bow

SPECIAL DELIVERY

Father Christmas with his sleigh full of gifts makes a happy Christmas celebration.

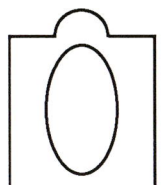

Pattern shown actual size

You will need:

To bake	1 oblong cake
Board	Allow 5 cm (2 inch) larger all round than cake

Special Effects: 42 medallions
Gifts and candy sticks to suit
1 Father Christmas
1 sleigh

FLORAL BELL

This unique and unusual idea of displaying a cake in a basket would be suitable for Christmas, anniversary or small wedding. This cake would look delightful in any colour combination.

You will need:

To bake	1 medium upright bell
Board	1 basket is used
Flowers	24 mountain primula 18 jasmine
Ribbons	29 loops 1 large florist bow

CHRISTMAS CHIMES

Celebrate your Christmas with this cake specially designed with simplicity in view. The crimper edge is emphasised with piped holly leaves and berries.

You will need:

To bake	1 medium upright bell-shaped cake
Board	Allow 5 cm (2 inch) larger all round than cake
Flowers	12 bunches of holly 17 native heath
Ribbons	1 large florist bow

NEW ARRIVAL

A novel way to say welcome to that very special bundle of joy. The sides of the cake have been kept very plain to show the painting to its best advantage.

You will need:

To bake	1 medium oval cake
Board	Allow 5 cm (2 inch) larger all round than cake
Flowers	7 daisies 10 rosebuds
Ribbons	1 metre (1 yard)

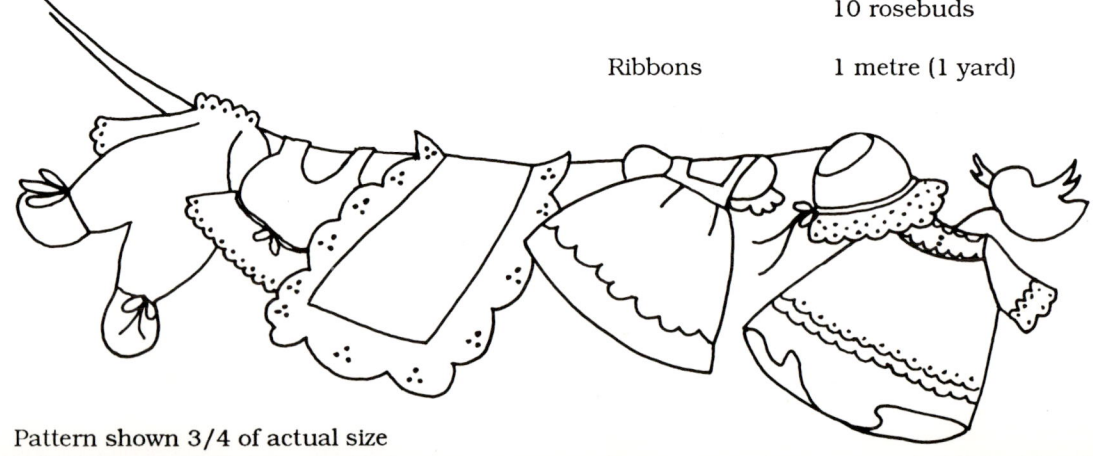

Pattern shown 3/4 of actual size

LITTLE ONE

Tiny sprays of blossom complement the beautiful baby and scroll on this truly elegant christening cake.

You will need:

To bake	1 medium oval cake
Board	Allow 5 cm (2 inch) larger all round than cake
Flowers	16 beauty bush blossoms 12 buds 42 cutter flowers
Special Effects:	1 scroll 1 baby in shawl

GRANDMA'S CUTIE

An exquisite cake just perfect for grandma's special grand-child. The smocking around the small bib is matched around the base of the cake. A teddy bear is flooded on the bib and finished off with a spray of flowers.

You will need:

To bake	1 medium hexagonal cake
Board	Allow 5 cm (2 inch) larger all round than cake
Flowers	21 bush orchids 9 buds 19 leaves
Ribbons	1 small bow

SWAN LAKE

An elegant cake for that special double christening. The dainty swan floats in front of twin clam shells amongst the pretty floral trim.

You will need:

To bake	1 medium oblong cake with the corners cut
Board	Allow 5 cm (2 inch) larger all round than cake
Flowers	14 cutter blossoms
Ribbons	1 metre (1 yard)
Special Effects:	1 crystal swan 2 moulded clam shells 2 tiny dolls

NURSERY TOYS

This cake has been designed to capture the attention of that special person in your life. The rocking horse and toys should be colourful for little eyes to admire.

You will need:

To bake	20 cm (8 inch) cake
Board	28 cm (11 inch)
Ribbon	1 metre (1 yard)
Special Effects:	Moulded rocking horse and teddies Gifts and candies

SLEEPY TIME

With a little imagination you will be able to make many scenes such as this to fit any occasion.

You will need:

To bake	20 cm (8 inch) round cake
Board	28 cm (11 inch) round
Flowers	10 tiny cutter flowers

Pattern shown 3/4 of actual size

ROCK-A-BYE BABY

A garland of flowers surround the hand-moulded cradle on this pretty christening cake. The lovely shaded effect has been achieved by spray painting the cake before attaching the flowers.

You will need:

To bake	1 medium oblong cake
Board	Allow 7.5 cm (3 inch) larger all round than cake
Flowers	24 fairy bells 9 leaves
Ribbons	1 metre (1 yard)
Special Effect:	1 cradle

WONDERFUL GIFT

The family of rabbits makes this cake a real treasure for your precious little one. This design would be suitable for a boy's or girl's christening or a toddler's birthday surprise.

You will need:

To bake	1 medium hexagonal cake
Board	Allow 5 cm (2 inch) larger all round than cake
Flowers	4 *Kurume* azaleas 7 rosebuds 40 cutter flowers 6 sprays of sweet rocket 12 tiny leaves
Ribbons	1 small bow 1 metre (1 yard)
Special Effects:	3 hand-moulded rabbits 1 bib

TINY BOOTIES

Royal iced booties are featured on this sweet, simple cake with a colour scheme that can be altered to suit either a boy or girl. The double frill on the edge has been sprayed to carry the soft colours through to the board.

You will need:

To bake	20 cm (8 inch) round cake
Board	28 cm (11 inch) round
Flowers	18 mountain primula 12 sprays of sweet rocket
Ribbons	7 bunches 1 metre (1 yard)

ANNIVERSARY FAN

This cake can be adapted for any anniversary. The simple arrangement of dog roses is ideal for the novice decorator.

You will need

To bake	1 fan-shaped cake
Board	Allow 5 cm (2 inch) larger all round than cake
Flowers	5 dog roses 8 sprays of lily-of-the-valley 8 star flowers 5 leaves 20 cutter flowers
Ribbons	6 bunches

SPARKLING DIAMOND

A special event needs a special cake. This cake with its *Phalaenopsis* orchids will add that finishing touch to a wonderful celebration.

60

Pattern shown actual size

You will need:

To bake	1 large diamond-shaped cake
Board	Allow 7.5 cm (3 inch) all round larger than cake
Flowers	6 *Phalaenopsis* orchids 12 mountain primula 6 sprays of sweet rocket 6 sprays of baby's breath 6 jasmine 9 leaves
Ribbons	6 bunches 3 metres (3 yards)

LOTUS BLOSSOM TIME

Lotus blossoms adorn the top of this elegant cake which can be used for any special occasion. Graduated shaded frills are used to acheieve the delicate colour harmony.

You will need:

To bake	1 medium oval cake
Board	Allow 5 cm (2 inch) larger all round than cake
Flowers	7 lotus blossoms 7 bunches *Bouvardia*
Ribbons	3 large bunches 3 small bunches

AUTUMN LEAVES

You can turn a round cake into a world of its own with the use of autumn leaves. This cake is sure to please the man in your life.

You will need:

To bake	20 cm (8 inch) round cake
Board	28 cm (11 inch) round
Flowers	22 ivy leaves in varying sizes
Special Effect:	1 scroll

CHERRY BLOSSOM LADY

This enchanting cake has a three dimensional look achieved by suspending the Japanese lady above the air-brushed panels. The lady was made from very finely rolled modelling paste and air-brushed to obtain the delicate shades. The simple spray of cherry blossom adds the finishing touch.

You will need:

To bake	23 cm (9 inch) square cake with corners cut
Board	Allow 7.5 cm (3 inch) larger all round than cake
Flowers	1 spray cherry blossoms
Ribbon	1.5 metres (1 1/2 yards)

Pattern shown actual size

JUST FOR YOU

A simply elegant cake which features colour under the broderie anglaise border to complement the elegant simplicity of the rose.

You will need:

To bake	medium hexagonal cake
Board	Allow 7.5 cm (3 inch) larger all round than cake
Flowers	1 large rose 6 leaves
Ribbons	1 bow 6 metres (6 yards)

RUBY ANNIVERSARY

Ruby red is the colour that symbolises forty years of marriage. Traditional red is carried through in the board, ribbon and flowers on this special cake.

You will need:

To bake	1 medium corner cut oblong cake
Board	Allow 7.5 cm (3 inch) larger all round than cake
Flowers	5 carnations 7 sprays of tiny tims 10 leaves
Ribbons	2 large bunches 3 small bunches 2 metres (2 yards)

GRADUATION DAY

This delightful floral arrangement featuring carnations, roses and daisies together with a scroll and mortar board make this a cake for that special graduation day.

You will need:

To bake	1 medium ocatagonal cake
Board	Allow 5 cm (2 inch) larger all round than cake
Flowers	5 carnations 6 roses 7 daisies 5 rosebuds
Ribbons	4 bunches 1 small bow
Special Effects:	1 mortar board 1 scroll

MY DIPLOMA

Designed to celebrate that special day in a young man's life, this cake has been balanced with a spray of delicately tinted blossom.

You will need:

To bake	1 medium oblong cake
Board	Allow 5 cm (2 inch) larger all round than cake
Flowers	2 bunches of tiny blossoms
Ribbons	2 metres (2 yards)

Pattern shown actual size

HOLY DAY

This cake sets the scene to celebrate a Communion or Confirmation Day. The tulle veil enhances the pretty girl in her embroidered frock.

You will need:

To bake	1 medium corner cut oblong cake
Board	Allow 5 cm (2 inch) larger all round than cake
Flowers	5 rosebuds 10 sprays of sweet rocket 4 tiny cutter blowers
Ribbons	2 small bunches 2 metres (2 yards) for bottom edge

Pattern shown actual size

COMMUNION DAY

Grapes and wheat are used on this cake to symbolise the bread and wine.

You will need:

To bake	20 cm (8 inch) square cake
Board	28 cm (11 inch) square
Flowers	36 bunches of piped grapes 6 ears of piped wheat Piped leaves to suit
Ribbon	3 tiny bunches 1 metre (1 yard) for side design

PRAYER BOOK

This cake is perfect in every detail for that special holy celebration day. The design has been kept simple so that the prayer book and double fuchsias are seen at their best.

You will need:

To bake	1 (8 inch) square cake
Board	1 (11 inch) square board
Flowers	11 double fuchsias 8 leaves
Ribbons	4 bunches of loops 1 metre (1 yard)
Special Effect:	1 bible with flooded cross

BON VOYAGE

Holiday time has arrived and your bags are packed for a wonderful trip. This cake fits the bill for holiday wishes.

You will need:

To bake	20 cm (8 inch) square
Board	28 cm (11 inch) square
Flowers	8 blossoms
	6 buds
Ribbons	10 sprays tiny forget-me-nots
Special Effect:	Luggage

WELCOME HOME

A large floral arrangement of Australian wildflowers enhance this unusual cake.

You will need:

To bake	1 Australia cake
Board	1 square board to suit size of cake
Flowers	1 waratah
	1 banksia
	6 sprays of wattle
	5 flannel flowers
	3 sprays of gumnuts
	1 spray of Christmas bells
	7 gum leaves
Special Effect:	1 scroll